Incomplete Knowledge

ALSO BY JEFFREY HARRISON

The Singing Underneath

Signs of Arrival

Feeding the Fire

An Undertaking (chapbook)

The Names of Things: New and Selected Poems (U.K.)

Incomplete Knowledge

POEMS

Jeffrey Harrison

Four Way Books
New York City

Distributed by
University Press of New England
Hanover and London

Editorial Office
Four Way Books
POB 535, Village Station
New York, NY 10014
www.fourwaybooks.com

Library of Congress Catalogue Card Number: 2005928314
ISBN-10: 1-884800-73-4
ISBN-13: 978-1-884800-73-3

Cover art: Cy Twombly, *Untitled*, 1970 [Rome], (oil, house paint, and oil/wax crayon on canvas, 136 x 159 inches). Cy Twombly Gallery, The Menil Collection, Houston, gift of the artist.

Cover design: KC Witherell/Hello Studio

This book is manufactured in the United States of America and printed on acid-free paper.

Four Way Books is a not-for-profit organization. We are grateful for the assistance we receive from individual donors, foundations, and government arts agencies.

This publication is made possible with public funds from the New York State Council on the Arts, a state agency.

Distributed by University Press of New England
One Court Street, Lebanon, NH 03766

[clmp]

We are a proud member of the Council of Literary Magazines and Presses.

ACKNOWLEDGMENTS

Grateful acknowledgment is made to the editors of the following publications in which these poems first appeared, sometimes in slightly different form:

Agni: "To Kenneth Koch," "Incomplete Knowledge"
The Gettysburg Review: "Fall Truce," "Unintended Elegy"
Hotel Amerika: "The Day My Mother Drowned,"
        "My Personal Tornado"
Image: "Coincidences," "Visitation Rights"
Iron Horse: "March First"
Leviathan Quarterly (U.K.): "Pale Blue City"
The Missouri Review: "Anniversary," "Happiness," "The Return,"
        "Visitation"
Ontario Review: "Breakfast with Dan"
The Paris Review: "Saint"
Ploughshares: "Age of Vanya"
Poet Lore: "Saturday, Late April"
Poetry: "Not Waking Up," "Poem for Roland"
The Southern Review: "God's Penis," "Thistle," "An Undertaking"
Tar River Poetry: "Inauguration of a House,"
        "My Worst Job Interview," "Vermeer Road Trip"
Western Humanities Review: "The Angel on the Table"
The Yale Review: "Fork," "The Names of Things"

*

"Saint," "Visitation," and "An Undertaking" also appeared in the chapbook *An Undertaking* (Haven Street Press, 2005).

"Fork" was reprinted in *Poetry: An Introduction*, fourth edition, and *The Bedford Introduction to Literature*, seventh edition, both edited by Michael Meyer.

"God's Penis" was reprinted in *The Pushcart Prize XXIX* (2005).

"Pale Blue City" was reprinted in *Air Fare* (Sarabande Books, 2004).

I am grateful to the John Simon Guggenheim Memorial Foundation
for a fellowship which enabled me to begin work on this collection,
and to the Peter S. Reed Foundation for a grant that helped me
to complete it; to The Frost Place and everyone associated with it
for their support and encouragement; to Karen Chase, Robert
Cording, Jessica Greenbaum, Peter Schmitt, and Baron Wormser,
for criticism which helped to shape these poems and this book; to
Michael Collier, Theodore Deppe, Alan Feldman, Edward Hirsch,
Eric Karpeles, Debra Nystrom, Stanley Plumly, Martha Rhodes,
Francesco Rognoni, William Wenthe, and Charlie Worthen, for
their helpful suggestions; and finally to Julie for seeing me through
the process of writing and revising these poems.

*

The Rilke quotation is from *Reading Rilke*, by William H. Gass
(New York: Alfred A. Knopf, 1999).

For my brother Andy,
in memory.

Charles Anderson Harrison
(1955-2002)

"That we were frightened by your death—no . . .
that your harsh death darkly interrupted us,
dividing what-had-been from what-would-be:
this is our concern; coming to terms with it
will accompany all our tasks."

—Rilke, "Requiem for a Friend"
(William H. Gass, trans.)

CONTENTS

I

Incomplete Knowledge 3

God's Penis 5

Pale Blue City 7

Fork 9

Inauguration Of A House 12

Vermeer Road Trip 13

Breakfast With Dan 15

Saturday, Late April 18

Thistle 20

My Worst Job Interview 22

My Personal Tornado 24

March First 26

To Kenneth Koch 27

Poem For Roland 30

Unintended Elegy 32

The Angel On The Table 34

The Day My Mother Drowned 35

II

Saint 39

An Undertaking

The Call 40

The Children 43

The Note 44

The Burial 45

The Apartment 47

His Socks 49

The Ring 51

The Note, 2 53

The Investigation	54
The Image	55
Confession	56
Plea	58
Visitation	60
Happiness	61
The Return	63
Age Of Vanya	65
Anniversary	66
Coincidences	68
Not Waking Up	73
Visitation Rights	74
Fall Truce	75
The Names Of Things	76

I

INCOMPLETE KNOWLEDGE

I am of those whose knowledge will always be
incomplete, who know something about the world
but not a whole lot, who will forever confuse
steeplebush and meadowsweet
but know at least by the shape of the flower
that it has to be one or the other.

Don't ask me the difference between
a pitch pine and a red, or even a Jeffrey,
though I know it's a pine, not a spruce or tamarack
(a.k.a. hackmatack, but what's a larch?).
The difference between a sycamore
and a plane tree? It's beyond me.

I've never had a real grip on
Japanese painting—the different periods and styles.
I don't even know that much about Dutch—
Vermeer of course, Rembrandt sure,
but could I distinguish a De Hooch from a Steen?
Do I even know how to pronounce their names?

I know next to nothing about what goes on
under the hood of a car, though I try to hide that fact
in the presence of mechanics. Herakleitus
(am I spelling that right?) said something
about how we hide our ignorance,
but I can't remember exactly what it was.

Birds, music, fishing, history, it's appalling
how limited my knowledge is.
I'm not even going to begin to list
all the books I haven't read.
I'm the antithesis of a Renaissance man,
spread so thin I hardly exist.

I have a friend who knows what seems like
close to everything. Certainly everything in the woods.
He was explaining to me the difference
between steeplebush and meadowsweet
(which I understood at the time but didn't retain,
as if it were the theory of relativity),

when I looked up and saw a jet whose trail
of fine white cloud kept disappearing, reappearing,
and disappearing again, and I asked why,
and, holding the meadowsweet in one hand
and the steeplebush in the other, he explained it.
And he wasn't bullshitting, either—he knew.

I'm not sure I even understand what it means
to know that much. Does all that knowledge
add up to some encompassing wisdom,
something beyond the sum of the names
and data, vast and unknowable? Unknowable
at least to me: I will never be like my friend.

I misplace facts as easily as my glasses,
so the world seems blurred for a while—
but then I find them, put them on, and go outside
to greet the ten thousand things (is that a Buddhist
or Taoist expression?), no less amazed
for my not being able to keep them straight.

GOD'S PENIS

As usual, I had my zealous eye
on Nancy Morris, the object both of my desire
and my envy: Professor Schneider's pet
in Seminar on Jewish Mysticism,
the one he'd stop his lectures for to offer
some private suggestion about her thesis.
Her seriousness masked her blonde, smooth beauty
in frown lines I'd been trying to read between
all term: was she a Goody Two-Shoes
or the sensualist I sometimes thought I glimpsed,
in the way, for instance, she was sucking
on her pen cap that day? I couldn't take
my eyes away, or keep my errant mind
from unbuttoning her cashmere cardigan.
But she, as always, had her blue-eyed attention,
her whole rapt being, focused on Schneider.
Was she in love with this hunched homunculus
older than his fifty years, almost a mystic himself,
who whispered quotations from Hassidic sages
in a German accent as thick as his gray beard?

During a lull in our discussion of the Kabbala
Schneider mentioned in passing an article
he'd seen in one of the scholarly journals
on God's penis. None of us had ever heard
anything crude pass through his oracular lips,
and before we knew whether to snicker
or take him at his startling word, his chosen pupil
gasped violently and bolted up like someone
suddenly possessed, with a force that sent
her chair clattering backwards. Everyone stared,
but she was speechless, grabbing at her neck.
"Are you choking?" I asked, remembering the pen cap,

and, as if this were a desperate game of charades,
she pointed at me—her first acknowledgment
of my existence. "Heimlich Maneuver!"
someone shouted, and Schneider lurched across the room,
and then he was doing it to her, hugging her from behind,
his hands clasped together under her snug breasts
and his pelvis pressing into her blue-jeaned ass,
closing his eyes and groaning with the exertion.

If it is true what Buber says, that no encounter
lacks a spiritual significance, then what
in God's unutterable name was this one
all about? Their long-awaited intimacy
nightmarishly fulfilled, or some excruciating twist
on "the sacrament of the present moment"?—
a phrase I remembered but couldn't have told you
where in the syllabus of mystic intimations
it came from. I couldn't have told you
anything: there was nothing but their dire embrace
wavering with the luminous surround
of a hallucination—and something inside me
rushing out toward them, silently pleading
"God, don't let her die!" The answer came,
torpedoing through the air and ricocheting
with a smack against the framed void of the blackboard.
Relief and embarrassment flooded the room
while the girl who had choked on God's penis
looked around astonished, as though she'd just returned
from a world beyond our knowing.

PALE BLUE CITY

(December 31, 2000)

I've never seen it like this: from up here
the sun sinking fiery on the horizon,
but down there it has already set, and the city,
laid out on its recognizable island,
is a beautiful pale ash blue
because of the snow and the evening.
The streetlights are already lit
but it isn't dark yet, everything is still
visible in the city where we once lived,
but long ago, and now it's all small:
the tiny paired towers of the Trade Center,
midtown stacked up like a digital mountain,
the George Washington Bridge with its festoon
of white Christmas lights, Central Park
an azure band. It's too far away to see
the copper roofs of Morningside Heights,
their green subsumed in the blue
of memory, or covered by the snow
that shut the city down our first year
together, people skiing down Broadway,
everything muffled as we looked down
from our window, already seeing it all
from above, but not from as far away
as this, the lights glittering, as if
through a liquid. I want it all to stay
just like this, I wish I could give you
this pale blue city under the glass
of a plane window like a snowglobe,
all of New York and our time there
held in your hand. But the plane
is moving on, the city slips away . . .
and now it's getting dark, the landscape
turns as black as space, and the orange

7

lights of other cities slide underneath
in spidery galaxies—as if light-years
separated us from that era. And yet
I try to hold it inside me as the plane
begins its descent toward our present
life together. Here: take it
before it disappears.

FORK

Because on the first day of class you said,
"In ten years most of you won't be writing,"
barely hiding that you hoped it would be true;
because you told me over and over, in front of the class,
that I was "hopeless," that I was wasting my time
but more importantly yours, that I *just didn't get it*;
because you violently scratched out every other word,
scrawled "Awk" and "Eek" in the margins
as if you were some exotic bird,
then highlighted your own remarks in pink;
because you made us proofread the galleys
of your how-I-became-a-famous-writer memoir;
because you wanted disciples, and got them,
and hated me for not becoming one;
because you were beautiful and knew it, and used it,
making wide come-fuck-me eyes
at your readers from the jackets of your books;
because when, at the end of the semester,
you grudgingly had the class over for dinner
at your over-decorated pseudo-Colonial
full of photographs with you at the center,
you served us take-out pizza on plastic plates
but had us eat it with your good silver;
and because a perverse inspiration rippled through me,

I stole a fork, slipping it into the pocket of my jeans,
then hummed with inward glee the rest of the evening
to feel its sharp tines pressing against my thigh
as we sat around you in your dark paneled study
listening to you blather on about your latest prize.
The fork was my prize. I practically sprinted
back to my dorm room, where I examined it:
a ridiculously ornate pattern, with vegetal swirls

and the curvaceous initials of one of your ancestors,
its flamboyance perfectly suited to your
red-lipsticked and silk-scarved ostentation.

That summer, after graduation, I flew to Europe,
stuffing the fork into one of the outer pouches
of my backpack. On a Eurail pass I covered ground
as only the young can, sleeping in youth hostels,
train stations, even once in the Luxembourg Gardens.
I'm sure you remember the snapshots you received
anonymously, each featuring your fork
at some celebrated European location: your fork
held at arm's length with the Eiffel Tower
listing in the background; your fork
in the meaty hand of a smiling Beefeater;
your fork balanced on Keats's grave in Rome
or sprouting like an antenna from Brunelleschi's dome;
your fork dwarfing the Matterhorn.
I mailed the photos one by one—if possible
with the authenticating postmark of the city
where I took them. It was my mission that summer.

That was half my life ago. But all these years
I've kept the fork, through dozens of moves
and changes—always in the same desk drawer
among my pens and pencils, its sharp points
spurring me on. It became a talisman
whose tarnished aura had as much to do
with me as you. You might even say your fork
made me a writer. Not you, your fork.
You are still the worst teacher I ever had.
You should have been fired but instead got tenure.
As for the fork, just yesterday my daughter

asked me why I keep a fork in my desk drawer,
and I realized I don't need it any more.
It has served its purpose. Therefore
I am returning it to you with this letter.

INAUGURATION OF A HOUSE

Right away the ill omens begin:
the seller's lawyer has a blood-stained eye.
Then a drunk driver knocks the mailbox down,
and I kill a snake in the basement,
its mottled body writhing on the slab.
All before we've even moved in.

Is this an initiation? We try to dispel any evil
by sprinkling kosher salt in all the corners,
then set to work to make the house
our own. All the old knob-and-tube wiring
is ripped out of the horsehair walls
and replaced with virgin Romex.

I spackle and repaint, bash my knuckles
lugging boxes in, struggle with molly
and toggle bolts, and pinch my thumb with pliers,
raising a blister as dark as a Concord grape.
The plumber gets our one toilet running
but warns, "She's going to sweat like a pig."

The house doesn't begin to feel like ours
until we're making love in it, on this bed
we had to dismantle to get upstairs,
and under this roof that needs repairs.
We're trying not to think about that now,
making sure instead that this is good

for both of us, making it last,
tasting the wet salt on each other's skin,
here among these boxes stacked
like sandbags against disaster or attack,
until these walls I've patched
absorb our cries and take us in.

VERMEER ROAD TRIP

for Bob Cording

We left our wives and children and headed south
for Washington, two middle-aged men
who could have gotten ourselves into trouble

had we been looking for adventure
instead of something like its opposite:
the apotheosis of the ordinary,

moments held like a pearl in a balance
or drawn out and poured like a stream of milk
from an earthenware pitcher.

We talked about Vermeer, and about poetry,
though I made us promise never to write poems
about Vermeer—there were already enough of those . . .

a promise which I seem to be breaking now.
But this isn't really about Vermeer,
it's about the trip down and the trip back

when we stopped in New York to see
the handful of Vermeers at the Met and Frick
and have a quick sandwich on Madison.

In the closed-off chamber of the car, seen through
that camera obscura at high speed,
our own lives seemed as tranquil as Vermeers,

anything that might resemble drudgery
refined to sacrament, everything messy
or violent left outside the frame,

the way Vermeer left out the chaos
of his household, the stink of chamber pots,
the needs and noise of his eleven children.

We talked about our wives as though
they were as young and opalescent
as the "Girl in a Turban"

or spent whole portions of their days
just standing in the sanctifying light
that slanted through a window's leaded panes—

as though we lived in a world where no one
aged or raised his voice in anger,
where nobody got sick and died (or worse),

where everything could be held
in hushed suspension
only by our staying out of the picture.

BREAKFAST WITH DAN

Dan meets me by the cube at Astor Place
and shoves me into the street by way of greeting,
a violent enthusiasm being one of the symptoms
of his Asperger's syndrome, a kind of autism
turned inside-out. He says we can't eat
at any of the fucked-up yuppie bistros around here
because they've banished him, so we start walking east
on St. Mark's, on our way to what he calls
his favorite "wackro-biotic restaurant."
He talks nonstop as he takes us block after block,
into the alphabet streets, blurting verbiage
at passersby, shouting manic greetings
at all the street people (whom he knows
by name), and dipping into conversations
of wary pedestrians going in our direction.
In the middle of his monologue I slip him
fifty bucks to spare him the indignity
of asking me later, this furtive exchange
like a drug deal having become
standard practice for our sporadic meetings,
the under-the-table entry fee, so to speak,
to his buzzing world. Back when we were both
card-carrying expatriate artists, we breathed
the same rarefied air, but now that we're
back in the "United States of Ambivalence,"
I'm a foreigner in his gritty domain,
a slightly edgy tourist trying not to stand out.
When half a block later Dan flailingly accosts
a twenty-something brother with a lopsided face
and hair sprouting in a thousand tiny braids,
they palaver in a language I only half understand,
though it's clear that Dan is giving him shit
for not showing up at some Nader benefit.

These are the grass roots, sprouting like weeds
through cracks in the worn granite slabs
of lower Manhattan's pavement, and Dan
has taken on politics with the same fervency
he brought to researching his own disease
and diagnosing himself: he read everything
he could get his agitated hands on until he knew
more than any doctor. And now he knows precisely
what is wrong with America, and he tells me,
railing against its megalomania as we
enter our destination, an oxymoronic
greasy-spoon-health-food diner. Dan cans his rant
for exactly long enough to order the scrambled tofu
with a glass of beet juice, and for me to order
twelve-grain toast and coffee, then resumes. I'm just
nodding and smiling at his riffs between bites of toast
whose myriad grains scrape the lining of my throat
like an abrasive, when a schlumpy young woman
who's been eyeing us from across the room
comes over looking earnestly at Dan. I'm thinking,
What kind of woman would be drawn to someone
so apparently "out there," though I'm the first to admit
he has a ragged, jumpy magnetism. She says,
"I couldn't help hearing your conversation"
and asks Dan if he thinks she'd be throwing
her vote away if she voted for Nader.
Dan sighs and begins explaining that the Democrats
have New York in the bag anyway, but she
doesn't understand, and Dan gets more animated,
and I can see it coming but have no way
of stopping it, and suddenly he is on his feet announcing,
"This is what we're up against in America!
This girl"—pointing at her and addressing

the entire motley clientele of the restaurant—
"doesn't know what the Electoral College is!"
and on and on, and I'm trying to calm him down,
but he shakes off my hand and continues haranguing
the girl as she coweringly pays and runs out.
And now the owner—a Jamaican in a striped apron—
comes out shouting at Dan to shut up or leave,
and Dan says, "Oh, yeah?" and picks up his plate
and frisbees it across the room, scrambled tofu
flying in every direction until the plate crashes
against the wall and falls shattering to the floor.
Dan has a goofy smile on his face, like he's
both ashamed and proud of what he's done,
but he's not moving, and the owner is yelling
and jabbing at the buttons on the phone, so I
throw down a twenty and grab Dan and yank him
toward the door, calling "Sorry" over my shoulder—
then we're off running through the hubbub of
late morning in lower east side New York,
and Dan says to me through heaving breaths,
"For God's sake, I can't take you anywhere."

SATURDAY, LATE APRIL

On a day like this, the sky sponged blue
as if starting afresh with spring's late
but finally emphatic arrival, the cool air
warmed just enough by the sun to let us
comfortably peel away our sweatshirts,
on such a day you can almost forget
what you've been through—the dark months
of winter, recent weeks of chilly rain, deaths
and illnesses, your own murkier blues—

especially if you have the proper mindless
activity . . . like moving a pile of dirt
from one place to another. So I'm lucky, I guess,
that when I wanted to smooth out a depression
in my yard, to give the kids a better place
to toss the baseball, the dump truck left too much loam.
At first it seemed like another problem: How
am I going to unburden myself of this dirt?
But it turns out my friend down the road needs topsoil,

and he borrows an old pickup truck and comes over
with his kids, who are pals with mine,
and the six of us spend this clarion afternoon
shoveling the dark moist soil teeming with earthworms
in and out of the truck and driving back and forth
between our house and theirs, the kids riding in back,
laughing, throwing mudballs at street signs
and mailboxes, missing every time—and all the while
we're listening to the Red Sox on the radio.

Sometimes this is all it takes, moving a pile
of screened loam on spring's first gorgeous day,
the Sox going into extra innings with the Yankees
and finally winning it in the twelfth, all of us

cheering around the battered truck (it's only April—
we can still be hopeful), our chore done, shivering
with chill and contentment, our sweatshirts
back on as the sun goes down behind the leafless trees
like a glowing, slow-motion home run.

THISTLE

They've begun to overrun
the ferns, tall grass,
and weedy flowers between
the driveway and the woods,
their prickly heads
bulging with seed
turning to thistledown,
so I pull on the thick
leather gloves and grab
the silver-bladed trowel
by its ash haft.

"Pernicious weeds,"
the field guide says, as if
they were emissaries
of the devil, thorny ranks
in spiked helmets tufted
with purple plumes,
spreading like sin
through the Saint Johnswort
and pearly everlastings—
an allegory of flowers
I can't believe in.

And yet I might as well
be humming "Onward
Christian Soldiers"
as I attack them
with savage zeal.
I need, it seems, something
to be at war with,
and this season it's
these medieval weeds

beloved of bees
for their sweet nectar.

I yank the tall stalks
until my bare forearms
are stippled with a pink
rash and my eyes sting
with the tiny, invisible
thorn-pricks of salt,
the spiny bract
of some ancient hatred
bristling inside me,
more difficult to eradicate
than thistle.

MY WORST JOB INTERVIEW

had to be the one where I was naked.
Well, it was a phone interview, so the dean
couldn't see me, but I think he could tell from my
quavering voice that he'd taken me by surprise
if not that he'd caught me just as I'd
stepped out dripping from the shower. Is now
a good time? No, why don't you call back
when I'm on the toilet and then we can really
get down to business. What I really said
was foolishly yes as I managed to dry myself
but not to get dressed because the phone cord
wasn't long enough to stretch to the bureau.
It was almost 11:00 on a January night
and I was shivering from both cold and nerves
as he told me he wanted to follow up
on our "colloquy" from the day before:
he understood it had come at the very end
of a long day that included interviews
with half a dozen people, and he just wanted
to give me the opportunity to express
more clearly my "pedagogical concerns."
"Excuse me?" I managed, as the first drop
of frigid sweat slid from my armpit and trickled
down my pallid side and all the way along my leg
to my fidgeting foot. My teaching philosophy.
My mind was then as bare of philosophy
as my anatomy was of vestments,
but I stammered some desperate answer,
only to be confronted like a frightened animal
with the bludgeon of "Why do you want this job?"
I couldn't remember why I wanted it
or if I even did, I babbled like someone
with a gun to his head instead of a phone,

spilling my inarticulate guts about how
I'd always been lousy at interviews, how everyone
always said, "Just be yourself," but what they wanted
was for you to be somebody else and goddammit
I couldn't be anybody except myself,
and if that wasn't good enough then for God's sake
hire somebody else, some bullshit artist
who is good at interviews and can soliloquize
in the latest critical gibberish,
but with me what you see is what you get,
I stand here as it were naked before you.
Or something along those lines. He thanked me
for my unadorned candor and said good-bye.
"There's not a chance in hell I'll get this job,"
is what I told my wife before climbing
back in the shower to scour myself
of the whole experience, the steaming water
pouring in torrents over my grateful body.

MY PERSONAL TORNADO

is what my mother called
the sudden storm that ripped
through the yard and left
the neighbors untouched. Trees
uprooted and thrown to the ground
like dying giants, the corner of the house
crushed. I thought of the phrase again
when my aunt's husband was hit
by a series of strokes
and her youngest son was diagnosed
with AIDS. They died the same year,
and it was only a few more
before she succumbed to cancer.

Heart attacks, car accidents,
a lump in the breast felt
in the morning shower, the maelstrom
of sudden unemployment, revelation
of a spouse's faithlessness,
vortex of divorce—we all have one,
it's just a matter of when it hits
and how. Even a mild depression,
a pocket of low pressure, something
as tiny as a tick bite is enough,
and the sky takes on that greenish cast
like fruit rotting before it ripens,
the clouds tinged with jaundice.

Then this mere twist in an overcast
existence starts spinning and
there is no stopping it, this beast
of wind that sucks you into
the updraft of its hungry funnel

or screaming peels the roof
off your life and leaves you
cowering naked in its roar. . . .
What mine might be I'm almost
afraid to imagine, lest I call it
into being: whirling demon,
spiral tentacle, coil of storm—
do not touch down just yet.

MARCH FIRST

No news today—the newspaper got buried
in the mountain of snow the plow left,
and I think I won't turn on the radio,
so that for one day at least I won't know
what's happening in the world, except right here:

a fresh eight inches on the shed roof,
the pine boughs almost sadly weighed down,
but the upslanting branches of the pin oaks
looking oddly more buoyant in their white highlights.
Today I'm more like the pines, I'm afraid,

drooping a little, unable to shake it off
the way a pine branch suddenly springs up
in a brief explosion of shed snow.
Over seventy inches this winter
the newspaper said the other day—

but I don't even want to think about the newspaper,
that "tissue of horrors," as Baudelaire called it,
though I like imagining it under the snow.
Maybe the kids will dig a fort and find it,
still folded in its orange plastic bag,

still dry, the pages cold when they open it
to read the comics in the aqua light
that filters through the snow fort's snowy walls.
Or maybe we won't find it until all
the snow has melted and we've long

gone on to other news. And there it will be
on the brown, flattened-down grass,
next to a plastic bone the dog had lost,
its sodden pages finally able to tell us
what happened today.

TO KENNETH KOCH

I should say something to you
Now that you have departed over the mountains

How lucky that I ran into you
When everything was possible

—*from* New Addresses

Yesterday I was leafing through the *Times*
and saw your face suddenly
fifteen years younger smiling up
from the obituary page and stopped
breathing for a second and didn't answer
the question Julie was calling from upstairs
but after I started breathing again called
back to her that you had died as if
that were the answer to her question.
I don't know if you can hear me
where you are now or whether you
will get this at your new address
(it is an affectation to address the dead
one literal-minded poet once told me)
but reading your poems I know anything
is possible, and you addressed everything
with contagious ebullience:
my first and best teacher, who let me
into Imaginative Writing not because
the poems I showed you were any good
but because as you said in front
of the entire class that first day
there were so many of them! —and I was too
happy to be humiliated, proud to be the only
freshman of the chosen twelve, and I have
always been grateful and of course
you were right about the poems.

After I read the article, Julie and the kids and I
drove to Fenway Park (the Sox were playing
the Tigers). It was a weird murky day,
the sun shining weakly with an eerie light
through a sallow haze that the radio told us
was smoke from forest fires in Quebec.
I thought about you during the game—
how I was such a small part of your life
but you were a big part of mine, especially
those years at Columbia which have stayed with me
all this time, how we were both from Cincinnati
and I always liked to think that meant something
even though it didn't mean that much
but I still remember when I told you
you halted in surprise on the way out of
Hamilton Hall. I remember your office
on the fourth floor, looking through the window
at pigeons flirting on the ledges as you read
my poems or wrote a letter of recommendation
at tremendously high speed and then
read it aloud to me while I thought
Is anyone going to believe this? but it
and others like it got me to Paris
and a few less exciting places like
graduate school. And after that I didn't
see you as often but when I did was always
floored by the vigorous way you looked
at the world, like the time I showed you
a colossal elm with twisting limbs and you said
it was like a complicated stanza pattern
you'd like to write in. When something big happened
like a double play or a home run I'd come
awake to the crowd's cheers and wonder
if there was anyone else in the ballpark

thinking of you. The flag was at half-mast
for Ted Williams (and of course, I thought, for you).

But it was the exuberance of the crowd
in the later innings that was most like you,
and when the wave started going around
the Fenway grandstands I held
my sadness in check and joined the celebration,
throwing my arms up with all the others
as that many-tentacled surge moved
with the energy of one of your poems,
coming to a brief stop at the left field stands
and then reappearing in the center field bleachers,
leaping invisibly across the synapse
of the Green Monster, like your leaps
which always amazed me, and then it
came toward us again and we laughed
in anticipation and rose up cheering
with everyone around us as the wave
moved past us and we sat down
until our turn came to be part of it again.
The sun was still trying to come through
and sometimes pierced the haze as if
to look down on the stadium—Kenneth,
life seemed to burst from you like light
from the sun, and if now that sun is gone
I have your poems that never stop asking,
"So what is the ecstasy
we are allowed to have in this one life?"

POEM FOR ROLAND

(Roland Flint, 1934-2001)

This morning I came downstairs and found my seven-year-old
reading your last book, which I'd left on the table,
her blue eyes calm and serious, her lips quietly moving.
She'd misread the cover, taken it on trust: Easy Poems—
expecting maybe something like Shel Silverstein,
though she knew from me that poems don't have to rhyme.

When I explained her mistake, that the title was just *Easy*,
she kept going, all the way through the poem she was reading,
without asking any questions. I didn't remind her
that she'd met you once, because I didn't want to tell her
you had died. I wanted instead to tell you
about this moment, to hear your ample laugh. . . .

When Eliza set the book down thoughtfully and turned
back to her cereal, a bowl (no joke) of Life,
I picked up the book and opened to the poem
in which you witness your neighbor, a young father,
impatiently teaching his six-year-old to ride a bike
by telling him over and over he's doing it wrong.

Then I remembered what you could never forget:
the death of your own son when he was six.
And here was Eliza, only one year older now,
a child, like the boy with his gleaming new bicycle,
you wouldn't have been able to look at without thinking
of Ethan, who today would almost be my age.

Yet I knew you would have laughed all the more loudly
to see Eliza in her butterfly pajamas
reading your book, whatever its title,

your delight erupting from a place far down in you
where your grief lived, and deepened by the knowledge
that she had understood what she'd read

in her own way, that she had not made a mistake:
the poems *are* easy for her now, but won't be later.

UNINTENDED ELEGY

(Leslie Furth, 1957-2004)

It's a Van Ruisdael sky today, big puffy clouds
blowing by, and even a few large birds, probably buzzards,
soaring up there, tiny, their shriveled heads
only a remote idea, as if beauty depended
on keeping one's distance, or on wearing the proper
sunglasses, which lend an opalescent glow
to the slow-motion turbulence at the edges
of clouds when the sun is behind them.
A jet roars quietly through a blue

opening, its nose glinting with sunlight,
but its wake of vaporous pollution
remains invisible for now, allowing me
not to dwell on it. Sometimes I worry about
what kind of decay might be eating away
at the house beneath its supposedly
protective shell of vinyl siding—
battalions of insects gnawing through sodden wood?—
but it's too nice a day to think about that.

Then I remember—Oh God: Leslie, dying
three thousand miles away in California,
her eyesight all but gone, the cancer having taken
the faculty she needed most to do the work she loved
in art history. Once, on the phone, she asked me
to help her find a metaphor for her disease
so she could visualize her fight against it.
"I just can't identify," she said good-naturedly,
"with all the military imagery."

That was a few months ago, and now it's too late
for metaphors, or even phone calls. If I
could give her anything, it would be this day

of early spring in her native Massachusetts:
the daffodils already shriveled on their tough stems,
but the crab apples full of unopened blossoms
like pink, compact berries, the *sweet sweet sweet*
of the cardinal, the blue jay's vocal spear—
things she might find beautiful, if she were here.

THE ANGEL ON THE TABLE

She's losing her memory, isn't sure
who I am, is bothered by small things
like where that angel made from doilies
came from, the one she made herself
in the home's craft class. I remind her, but she
forgets again, and in a minute asks again,
as if she's just noticed it for the first time.

The body is a doily twisted into a cone.
A doily cut and folded forms the wings.
The head is a Styrofoam ball, the hair a tuft
of cotton, the halo a gold pipe cleaner.
As simple and innocent as something
a child would bring home from school,
and in fact my daughter made one like it.

But this angel is a small torment to her,
perched on the table beside the photographs
of people she no longer recognizes—
but that doesn't bother her. It's the angel
she eyes with suspicion, even fear.
Where did it come from, what is it doing there,
what on earth does it want from her?

THE DAY MY MOTHER DROWNED

It was one of those humid late winter days
that seem depressed somehow: fog snagged
in the leafless trees, hanging over old snow that lay
like decomposing foam rubber. And then our grandmother
was saying she couldn't find our mother,
her voice edged with an infectious desperation.

We started searching for her, all over the house,
the garage, the yard, the barn, our grandmother calling
Anne? Anne? into the woods, the thick fog
absorbing her quavering voice, then her.
My brother and I called too, *Mom* then *Mommy*,
feeling smaller with each call, whimpering a little.

Then our grandmother staggered back into the yard
blubbering that she'd found our mother's footprints
going into the lake, but there were no tracks
coming out again—she kept repeating that.
We didn't understand until she said
the word "drowned," drawing it out in a howl

that rose in pitch, taking our breath
with it, our grandmother's hysteria
mounting until it avalanched in sobs
like clumps of wet snow sliding
off the house's steep roof as our bodies
slackened and the sky went spinning black.

Just then our mother appeared through the mist
like an apparition, in her yellow slicker.
"We thought you were dead," our grandmother wailed.
"For Pete's sake, Mother, I was just taking a walk."
My brother and I just stood there, unable to expunge
the world we'd imagined without her.

II

SAINT

I find you where I found you years ago,
stone saint from 15th century France
whom I can count on always to be here
in this church-like corner of the museum.

Forgive me for not visiting in so long.
Now I want to tell you everything
that has happened to me since I last saw you,
but I can see by your deeply shadowed eyes

that you already know. I place myself directly
in your warm and comprehending gaze.
I want to lose myself in the thick folds
of your stone robe, in the ripples of your beard.

The smooth dome of your bald head
is the firmament of your compassion.
Put down your heavy book and lay your hand
gently on top of my head. Pray for me.

AN UNDERTAKING

For Andy, in memory.

The Call

The undertaking
of his suicide

a task
beyond understanding

exerts its force
like a huge dark moon

we hadn't known before
but whose pull

will never release us
the way he took himself

forcibly under

        *

If I return to that night
maybe I can stop

returning to that night
every night

the phone's ring
tearing me from sleep

my father's voice
saying he's dead

my mother's screams
piercing me

my head still able to speak
from somewhere above

my hunched body

        *

we held each other against it
but it would not let go

three times shitting it out
but it was still inside me

then the second call
my father saying yes

he did it himself
and I asked how

and he (not wanting
my mother to hear)

told me to guess
I got it on my second guess

and he said "unh-hunh"
as if it was a normal conversation

only more quietly
tentatively

and I wailed Why
did he do *that*?

and he said I don't know

    *

. . . downstairs to make tea
as if we were still ourselves

the sour taste it left
in my mouth

as I lay in the dark
like death I thought

wind rattling the windows
freezing rain

hissing against the panes
my cold cold feet

my brother

The Children

The next day, Sunday morning,
we didn't tell the kids right away

but let them eat their cereal
and read the funnies and sports page,

spread out on the kitchen table,
without knowing.

I thought of the scavenger hunt
he made for them one summer,

his silly rhyming clues that had them running
through fields and woods.

We looked hard at their faces,
knowing it would be the last time

we would see them like that,
wishing we could keep them there, suspended

in that other world. We waited a long time—
maybe half an hour—before asking them

to come and sit with us in the living room.

The Note

The police took it as evidence,
but the detective said the coroner
had a photocopy,
so I called him from my parents' house,

and sitting in the office
which had been my brother's room
I watched his suicide note
feed through the fax machine—

I've had a really
good life. Thank you
to everyone who was
a part of it.

—in his big, innocent
unconnected letters.
Like a note saying
he'd gone out for a walk

and would never be back . . .
that shift in tense
from something ongoing
to something gone.

The Burial

My tears have been my meat day and night...

As we arrived at the cemetery
I thought about how he and I
worked on the lawn crew there
two summers in a row.
Seven hundred acres: you never
finished cutting the grass.
If there was a funeral nearby
we stopped working and stood
awkwardly around our mowers
until it was over.

In the midst of life we are in death...

He loved to tell stories
about the characters on our crew—
old Joe, who chewed tobacco
and smoked at the same time,
whose wife intercepted his paychecks
before he spent them on booze;
and "Flash," who'd been struck
by lightning and looked
nervously over his shoulder
if the sky darkened.

a sheep of thine own fold, a lamb of thine own flock

After the priest read the rites
and the box of ashes,
wrapped like a gift,
had been placed in its recess,
some of us dropped roses in,
and the children came forward
with drawings and notes
and dropped them in.
Looking up, I caught the faltering eye
of a workman waiting nearby.

. . . yet even at the grave we make our song . . .

The Apartment

We stopped at Starbucks on the way—
a stalling tactic, but also
a mistake: by the time we reached
his door, our nerves screamed
in caffeinated panic.

Going in, what freaked me most
were the piles of black powder
on the beige carpet. What
was this stuff—something forensic
the police hadn't cleaned up?

They were everywhere,
these mounds, black and malignant,
with a bitter smell we almost
recognized. I couldn't do anything
until I vacuumed them up.

Then we bagged up clothes,
emptied the kitchen shelves,
packed pots and pans in boxes,
moving him out, moving ourselves
into a life without him.

Ruthless, we swept
the contents of the medicine chest
into a black garbage bag,
tossed his cross country skis
into a dumpster, never wept.

I found the bottle of Zoloft,
counted out the pale blue pills,
and did the math:
twenty-nine days.
I wondered if they killed him.

Even the most innocent detail—
a banana refrigerator magnet
holding a nephew's drawing—
felt tainted, as if
by that black powder,

which turned out to be—
why hadn't we recognized it?—
coffee grounds
that had been scattered
to mask the smell.

His Socks

Starting with the tumulus
on the floor beside his dresser,
clean but not yet put away
(now never to be put away),
a cairn of soft rocks
at least two feet high,
though many of them were not
balled up into pairs
but loose, or tied to their mates.
There were more in the dresser,
more on the closet shelves,
nests of them, like litters
of some small mammal, sleeping—
or dead, like the litter
of newborn rabbits that froze
when we were kids.
We buried them in a shoebox.
In every box my father
and I went through, no matter
what it contained—old papers,
framed photos, cassette tapes—
there would always be
at least a few more pairs,
and the one who found them
would call to the other,
"More socks," in sad amazement,
or exasperated bafflement,
because, for the life of us,
we couldn't find an explanation.
And what might have seemed

one of his endearing foibles
we couldn't keep from seeing
as some dark obsession,
one more thing about him
we hadn't known, would never
understand. Who could need
so many socks? Nylon dress socks,
gym socks of white cotton,
gray wool hunting socks
with an orange band on top,
even a few, from deep
in a trunk, with name tags
our mother had sewn in
decades ago. Enough socks
for several lifetimes,
though his one life was over.
Socks whose heels were worn
to a tenuous mesh, others
in their original packaging,
but most somewhere between.
If I'd taken them all I never
would have had to buy
another pair, no matter
how long I lived. But I
kept thinking of his feet
and how those socks would
never warm them again.
I took only a few pairs—
loose-fitting cotton, gray—
to wear to bed on cold nights,
my own feet sheathed
in the contours of his.

The Ring

Sitting on the floor of his apartment
going through a pile of old papers—

lists of books and movies and CDs,
of slang expressions he found funny,
notes on market strategies, on dating strategies,
old letters, articles on health, and one
on sexual positions, which I pocketed—

I found a plain white envelope
and almost tossed it in the trash,
before I saw his wedding ring inside.

Bless, O Lord, this ring to be a sign
of the vows by which this man and woman
have bound themselves to each other

—vows he broke twelve years before
with a suddenness that stunned us.

Something made me slip it on,
but I couldn't get it past the knuckle.
When I got home I had a jeweler alter it.

of the vows this man has made
to cherish the memory of his brother

I am constantly aware of this ring
as I am constantly aware of his death.

with steadfast love

I fiddle with it, twisting it
and pulling it over my knuckle, worrying
that it's too loose, that the jeweler
made it too big, that I will lose it—

though a friend who has always worn a ring
says that someday I will hardly notice it.

as long as I shall live

The Note, 2

After three days in Chicago,
my father and I sat in a hotel room
numbly flipping channels.

Then I said I was going to bed
and absently picked up
the spiral notebook

we'd found in his apartment
and had been using to make lists
of things we needed to do,

and the glossy gray cover caught
the light, and I saw it,
the impression of the note

(he must have torn a page out
and placed it on the cover
before writing his last words).

I tilted it back and forth
under the lamp
for my father to see—

the words appearing
and disappearing, visible
then gone.

The Investigation

There were some things I would never know—
I realized that, but I wanted to understand
as much as I could before I let it go.

I couldn't stop making phone calls to Chicago—
to his doctor, his insurance agent, his doorman;
the coroner, who told me more than I wanted to know;

to his psychiatrist, who made a show
of sympathy and dismissed out of hand
my speculations—but I wouldn't let them go.

The detective sounded weary, which was no
surprise: it was 2 a.m. He patiently explained
what he could, then sighed, "You'll never really know."

I weighed possibilities, made lists, wrote memos
to myself: was it spontaneous or planned—
and for how long? I couldn't let it go.

I kept calling my brother and sister to let them know
what I had figured out. Each time, they listened
but then told me what I had always known:
we would never understand. I had to let it go.

The Image

of your death
I will not put
into words
I will carry it
inside me
all my life
I will not
put it down
these details
I never wanted
I will keep
in the darkest
part of me
where only
I can see
a haunting
I can't shake
that shakes me
I who have
spent my life
making images
this time
I refuse
these words
are my promise
to you

Confession

Once, after school, I followed you
into the woods without your knowing,

hanging back while you ambled along
and, to my suppressed amusement, sang

one of your funny nonsense songs
to the Newfoundland lumbering beside you.

You never saw me. The farther I followed you
along the trail, the more I felt the wrong

of what I was doing. You were my older
brother, and I had no right to witness

your moments of vulnerability.
And it was perhaps for that same reason

that, later on, I hardly ever asked about
what I have come to think of only now

as your illness: the panic attacks that led you
to stop driving, and your small odd habits

that were probably symptoms
but which I chose to see as harmless quirks.

Crossing streets with you, I never turned around
as you hung back, never looked to see

what little ritual you were performing
to prepare yourself for the crossing.

I didn't want to embarrass you,
to cause you further pain. What pain

you suffered I had no idea: more than you
could bear, than I can bear to think about.

But I knew it was there. I preferred
(and, forgive me, still prefer) to think of you

as you were that day I followed you
and then had second thoughts and snuck away,

while you went deeper into the woods,
you and the dog alone with your singing.

Plea

Forgive me for the promises I've broken.
I wanted to commemorate your life,
to say what you were like—funny, soft-spoken—
to tell stories about you, to describe your laugh,
but I seem to have written only of your death.
Forgive me. I've placed your photo on my shelf.
I look into your eyes in disbelief.
Can I forgive you for killing yourself?

Forgive me for not calling you more often,
especially those last weeks of your life.
Forgive the silences, the words not spoken,
forgive these words too late to give relief,
the tears I've shed and haven't shed in grief.
Forgive me for always thinking of myself
and for not seeing that you needed help—
and I will forgive you for killing yourself.

I'd like to believe the words that were spoken
at your memorial: that you are safe
in heaven. But we are here, heartbroken.
Even if there is an afterlife,
it's closed to the living, whatever our belief.
No one can forgive me but myself,
I see that now. You can't lighten my grief.
But I can forgive you for killing yourself.

Andy, you who were unable to ask for help,
"Beloved Son, Brother, and Uncle" (your epitaph),
if you can hear me beyond the bounds of death:
I forgive you for killing yourself.

VISITATION

for my mother

Walking past the open window, she is surprised
by the song of the white-throated sparrow
and stops to listen. She has been thinking of
the dead ones she loves—her father who lived
over a century, and her oldest son, suddenly gone
at forty-seven—and she can't help thinking
she has called them back, that they are calling her
in the voices of these birds passing through Ohio
on their spring migration . . . because, after years
of summers in upstate New York, the white-throat
has become something like the family bird.
Her father used to stop whatever he was doing
and point out its clear, whistling song. She hears it
again: "Poor Sam Peabody Peabody Peabody."
She tries not to think, "Poor Andy," but she
has already thought it, and now she is weeping.
But then she hears another, so clear, it's as if
the bird were in the room with her, or in her head,
telling her that everything will be all right.
She cannot see them from her second-story window—
they are hidden in the new leaves of the old maple,
or behind the white blossoms of the dogwood—
but she stands and listens, knowing they will stay
for only a few days before moving on.

HAPPINESS

My grandmother lost her mind just in time
to miss my brother's suicide.
Sometimes I wonder if he had that in mind.

Among his notes (and there were many)
was a sheet of loose-leaf paper
with one handwritten word: "Granny"—

as if to say . . . I guess we'll never know.
The page is as blank as her mind,
but maybe that's the point somehow.

So that at Thanksgiving, there's no sign
from her that anything's amiss.
Thank God, we think, she's lost her mind.

In a strange way she seems happy—
"happier than she's ever been," we say.
She used to get upset and cry so easily.

"Tell me who that nice-looking young man is,"
she asks about my other brother
for the fourth time. Each time we answer

as if for the first time, knowing it won't be the last,
and she no longer notices
her mistake, or gets embarrassed.

So it surprises us when she says, "Someone's missing."
We look at one another and at her,
and at our empty plates, the moment passing

swiftly into vacant wordlessness.
Is this what it takes to be happy, to live
in the present, as all the sages suggest?

"Push me off a cliff when I get like that,"
my father says later. And what?—
deny him his last chance at happiness?

THE RETURN

Half-listening to the radio on my way
home from doing errands, I'm pulled out
of wherever I've been by the quick story
that ends the hour's news: a man from Portugal
is killed while traveling—I miss both how
and where, but in another country.
The Portuguese embassy contacts the family,

and a few days later the death certificate
arrives in the mail. The body is to follow.
I am already thinking of my brother,
how even after seeing his death certificate,
that stark finality in black and white,
I let myself imagine that some mistake
had been made, that he might just show up—

the way the Portuguese man, after four more days,
arrived not in a box but on his feet, perfectly
alive, walking right back into his life as if
nothing had happened, though everything had.
We never even saw my brother's body,
only a small carton of ashes—
how could we even be sure they were his?

Even in the hopeless weeks that followed,
dreams came to me like visitations.
In one, my brother sat with us at dinner
but seemed unable to speak. In another,
seeing my astonishment at finding him alive,
he explained the whole misunderstanding
and apologized for making us think he was dead.

How strange to think my dream came true
for others, far away. I know the agony

they went through, the days and nights like molten
lead, heavy and deformed, toxic with grief.
But then they saw their husband and father
return from the dead. For he was truly dead.
They had the paper to prove it, now proven wrong.

For no reason, they received a miracle
that was denied us, and they went running out
to greet him, hugging him and weeping hard
for joy as they had in grief, slapping themselves
to make sure they weren't dreaming. In my dream
I hugged my brother with a joy so uncontainable
it woke me up, and then he died again.

AGE OF VANYA

Three months after my brother's death,
I saw *Uncle Vanya* in New York.
Near the end of the play, Vanya says
he's forty-seven years old. I had forgotten that,
and the line caught me off-guard. Forty-seven
was my brother's age when he killed himself.
I wondered if there was something about being
forty-seven—the very beginning of growing old—
that makes a certain kind of person take
the measure of his life and find it wanting,
even unbearable. Did Andy feel that way?

A few years earlier, over Christmas, Andy and I
had watched *Vanya on Forty-Second Street* together.
We kept rewinding and replaying the scene
near the end of Act Three, fascinated
by Wally Shawn's performance of Vanya's tirade
and lamentation, which was terrifying
but somehow funny, mordant but pathetic.
I almost don't want to admit we were laughing,
yet I also hold our shared laughter dear.
Now I wonder how close Vanya was to suicide,
and when that possibility entered my brother's mind.

Approaching forty-seven myself now, I can say
it hasn't entered mine. And yet, some days
I have to remind myself my life isn't over,
that I am still, by some measure, young,
that I shouldn't give up and it isn't too late
to get something done. There could be decades ahead,
or at least the thirteen years that Vanya
gives himself. I tell myself it's just a phase,
as our elders used to say annoyingly
when we were teenagers. It's just the age of Vanya,
something to dread, something to get beyond.

ANNIVERSARY

Such a strange word, with its ring
of celebration, for something
like this. But there seems
to be no other.

November now,
and darkness bears down
earlier each day
with a physical weight.

For weddings, the first anniversary
is paper. I have filled pages
with words, but what good has it done?
For suicides, the first year is lead.

But when the day finally comes,
it isn't as bad as the weeks
leading up to it. We set
an extra place at dinner

and light a candle
to bring my brother's absence near.
And then we talk about him.
Words are all we have

to bring back the time
he taught a parrot,
in someone's house in France,
to say, "I farted,"

or how he renamed Prince
and Shine, our uncle's
yapping black toy poodles,
Shit and Shinola.

We're laughing now.
Someone looking in
from the darkness outside
might think we're celebrating.

COINCIDENCES

When I switch on the car radio,
a voice with the singing inflection
of an Indian is saying

that what we call coincidences
are really glimpses
of the cosmic harmony,

and I think of my sister weeping
on the other end of the phone
when I told her the story,

beginning with our older brother
who, five years earlier, called me up
from his apartment in Chicago

to tell me about this poet
from Minnesota he'd met
after her reading at the Art Institute.

He didn't read a lot of poetry,
and it was unusual for him
to be telling me about a poet,

and he seemed a little disappointed
that I hadn't heard of her,
but I told him that didn't

mean anything—that she
hadn't heard of me, either,
which he laughingly confirmed.

I saw him in Cincinnati that Christmas
and he had her book with him
and wanted me to read it,

but he wouldn't let me take it home
to Massachusetts so I had to
read it fast, but I liked it.

Then three years later (and two ago),
I met the poet at a book fair in Seattle,
not realizing right away

that she was the same poet,
but when I did, I told her the story.
She said she remembered my brother,

because it was so unusual
for anyone who wasn't a relative
or friend to actually buy a book

and talk to her after a reading.
She said he'd been sweet
and funny, which sounds like him.

I told my brother, too,
and I'm sure he was amused,
but I can't remember what he said.

A year later, he was dead.
I found the book in his apartment
among his not many books:

The Green Tuxedo, by Janet Holmes.
There were yellow post-its
next to particular poems,

with notes in his childlike
non-script: "True story."
I left them there and took the book.

It has the same dark aura
as his video of Sam Shepard's *True West*
or his bootlegs of the Grateful Dead.

I told Janet about Andy's death
and she wrote a nice note back,
but we were not in very close touch,

and another year went by before
I got an e-mail from her saying
that her husband's son by a previous marriage,

a widower with a teenage daughter,
was dating my divorced sister—
is dating my sister.

Wow, I think, what a strange
coincidence, and I wonder, the way
I used to wonder when I was younger

and less skeptical, if this could
mean anything. So I call my sister
and tell her the whole story,

and that's when she starts crying,
and I think it's because I'm talking
about Andy, and I say I'm sorry,

but she says no, it's because she
really likes this guy, and she had
already been thinking that Andy

had somehow sent him to her
because he wanted her to be happy
after the bad end of her marriage

and the shock of his suicide.
And I say *wow* out loud now, and I keep
wondering what is at work here.

Who knows what it is or what
will happen, but the voice on the radio
is talking about "quantum non-locality"

and how two particles that have come
into even the most glancing contact
and go off in different directions

are forever related, and if you know
where one of them is you know
where the other one is,

which makes me wonder about
my brother's non-locality
in relation to Janet, who I know

is now in Idaho—and whether,
from his non-locality, Andy
has anything to do with all this.

The radio guru seems to be saying
yes, that coincidences mark
a state of grace, and we are all

living inside the mind of God,
and I don't care if he is
promoting his newest book,

I roll my window down and toss
my skepticism out like a bad grape,
and despite all that can go wrong

in a lifetime and everything
awful that has already happened,
right now, at least, I believe him.

NOT WAKING UP

The ocean whose muffled explosions
put me to sleep last night also woke me
this morning, but not all the way,
and yesterday's blue shimmering expanse
has become today an unreflecting band
of milky green under a sky whose wash
of muted grays refuses to burn off—
Whistleresque, with here and there a white
scribble where a wave rumples over in foam.

All day I am some kind of daytime
sleepwalker, like the every-so-often
lone beachwalker whose place I take later,
trying to remember last night's dream
with my brother in it—nothing prophetic
about it, no sense of his being or having
been dead, only my brother again,
though all the details have been washed away
by the mind's equivalent of surf.

I wish I could remember it better, since this
is the only way I'm ever going to see him.
But even later, when the clouds knot up
into dark muscles, piling thunder
on the thunder of waves, and revealing in flashes
the sky's invisible arteries, nothing
in either world comes fully into focus,
except the steady pulsing of the lighthouse
blinking its warning to whoever is out there.

VISITATION RIGHTS

Two nights before what would have been
his fiftieth birthday, I dreamed my brother,
dead almost three years, came back
for our grandmother's funeral.

Of all of us grandchildren,
he was the best about visiting her.
She hadn't died, but that didn't stop me
from thinking, This should be allowed,

the dead should be able to come back
briefly, on important occasions
like a relative's funeral—
when we need them most.

It makes so much sense I wonder why
it wasn't part of the plan from the beginning—
just some visitation rights
with very strict rules, if that's what it takes.

I know, the dream was a visitation,
but I hardly remember the dream.
We were in the same room together,
talking as we had in life,

but I don't remember what we said.
And I didn't get to ask him why
he'd killed himself, or tell him
that our grandmother had never known,

saved by her dementia. And then it was over,
darkened, unrecoverable. I want
something more. One or two waking visions—
that's all I'm really asking for.

FALL TRUCE

I want to declare a truce with autumn,
to make a pact with the sumac's
scarlet plumage, with poison ivy
engulfing the trunks of trees in leafy flames:
I will no longer hate your devious beauty.

I have resisted the poplar's
yellow flickering, and looked away
from maples blazing orange against the sky,
not wanting to be taken in. I have despised
the darkness coming earlier each day.

But I must give up my grudge against fall.
I want to draft a treaty with ink squeezed
from the pokeweed's purple berries.
I need to give myself back to the season,
to stop blaming fall for my brother's suicide.

I must learn to take what autumn offers me:
the wild grapes whose sour skins
make me squint; the ferns turning lacy and pale;
the tawny pine needles gathered by roadsides
in soft windrows, like sea foam;

even the shivering November rains
glazing the naked trees. I will try to accept the leaves
that let go, and the parched russet lobes of the oaks
that hold longer. Raking them in a cold sweat,
I will breathe more deeply the incense of death.

THE NAMES OF THINGS

Just after breakfast and still
waking up, I take the path cut
through the meadow, my mind caught
in some rudimentary stage,
the stems of timothy bending
inward with the weight of a single
drop of condensed fog clinging
to each of their fuzzy heads
that brush wetly against my jeans.
Out on a rise, the lupines stand
like a choir singing their purples,
pinks and whites to the buttercups
spread thickly through the grasses—
and to the sparser daisies, orange
hawkweed, pink and white clover,
purple vetch, butter-and-eggs.
It's a pleasure to name things
as long as one doesn't get
hung up about it. A pleasure, too,
to pick up the dirt road and listen
to my sneakers soaked with dew
scrunching on the damp pinkish sand—
that must be feldspar, an element
of granite, I remember from
fifth grade. I don't know what
this black salamander with yellow spots
is called—I want to say yellow-
spotted salamander, as if names
innocently sprang from things
themselves. Purple columbines
nod in a ditch, escapees
from someone's garden. It isn't
until I'm on my way back
that they remind me of the school

shootings in Colorado,
the association clinging to the spurs
of their delicate, complex blooms.
And I remember the hawk
in hawkweed, and that it's also
called devil's paintbrush, and how
lupines are named after wolves . . .
how like second thoughts the darker
world encroaches even on these
fields protected as a sanctuary,
something ulterior always
creeping in like seeds carried
in the excrement of these buoyant
goldfinches, whose yellow bodies
are as bright as joy itself,
but whose species name in Latin
means "sorrowful."

Jeffrey Harrison is the author of three previous books of poetry, *The Singing Underneath* (1988), selected by James Merrill for the National Poetry Series, *Signs of Arrival* (1996), and *Feeding the Fire* (2001), as well as the chapbook *An Undertaking* (2005). In spring 2006, the Waywiser Press published *The Names of Things: New and Selected Poems* in the United Kingdom. He has received fellowships from the John Simon Guggenheim Memorial Foundation and the National Endowment for the Arts, as well as two Pushcart Prizes, the Amy Lowell Traveling Poetry Scholarship, and the Lavan Younger Poets Award from the Academy of American Poets. His poems have appeared in *The New Republic, The New Yorker, The Paris Review, Poetry, The Yale Review, Poets of the New Century,* and in many other magazines and anthologies. He has taught at several universities and schools, including George Washington University, Phillips Academy, where he was the Roger Murray Writer-in-Residence, and College of the Holy Cross. He is currently on the faculty of the Stonecoast MFA Program at the University of Southern Maine.